Seeds

of

Encouragement

Charles Filson

ISBN 979-8-89345-387-4 (paperback)
ISBN 979-8-89345-388-1 (digital)

Christian Faith Publishing
832 Park Avenue
Meadville, PA 16335
www.christianfaithpublishing.com

Printed in the United States of America

Contents

Believe

To be the best you have to believe
      And the best place to start is with you.
Believe that anything is possible
      And the impossible will come true.

Tell yourself "I can, I will"
      And believe it from the start.
Say to yourself "I deserve the best"
      And feel it in your heart.

Other people may put you down
      But you refuse to stop.
If you truly believe the person inside
      Will come rising to the top

Stand Alone

Though people desert you when trouble appears
    And your whole world seems a mess
Your inner strength is all you need
    To help you pass the test.

You may not feel the inner strength
    Because your mind is full of fear
But let go of doubt and soon you'll see
    Your courage will appear.

To know that you have conquered fear
    And faced troubles on your own
Sets you apart and shows the world
    You'll not be hurt by anyone.

You're in Control

We all have problems we have to face
      But they don't have to get us down.
We can laugh at troubles and conquer fear
      Whenever they're around.

There might be problems around the bend
      But there's no need to fear.
Just walk straight at it with head held high
      And your problems will disappear.

That's not to say there won't be times
      When your problems get out of hand.
That's when you call on your inner strength
      And get yourself back in command.

Belief

We have nothing to fear as long as we believe,
    But it has to come from within.
Show others you believe in what you do.
    Start feeling alive again.

Belief in yourself will go a long way
    To the life you see for yourself.
Helping others become the best they can
    Instead of going through life by themselves.

Believing in others as well as yourself
    Builds friendships that no one can shake.
Give it a try, it doesn't cost anything
    And see what difference it could make.

No Sacrifice

Giving of self so others may live
        Is the ultimate sacrifice.
It shows how far you'd go for a friend
        By giving up your life.

You have what you need to get you by.
        If they need it, you're willing to share.
They shouldn't have to scrimp and save
        So show them that you care.

We're on the earth for such a short time,
        Just merely passing through.
Though the way you've treated others in life
        Is what people will remember of you.

Better Than You Think

It isn't easy to see the world as you do
    And face life on your own,
But you carry with you an inner strength
    That has helped you carry on.

You've not given up when trouble appears.
    You refuse to let it win.
You're much stronger than you realize.
    You can compromise but never give in.

Each day will bring problems you have to face.
    But that's nothing new to you.
Just say to yourself "I'm better than them,"
    And there's nothing you can't do

No Comparison

You may have all the money in the world,
    Build monuments of stone,
But if you do nothing to help your fellow man,
    You're going to die alone.

The beggar you had no time for
    May not wear the finest clothes,
But he's wealthier in friends than you'll ever be
    Because of the life he chose.

He chose to give everything he owned
    To those who were most in need
While you squandered your money on frivolous joys,
    Spending on self and greed.

Pass It On

Some people go the extra mile
  To make others feel at home.
It doesn't cost them anything
  To see people are not alone.

Those that take this upon themselves
  Never seek glory or fame,
Never seek honor in any way,
  But they hope others will do the same.

They hope what they do will be passed on
  From one person to another,
And so continue endlessly
  'Til all people stand as brothers.

Rejoice

Some find pleasure just by being alive.
     Life is a wonderful thing.
There's joy and laughter in everyday living
     With all the magic it brings.

Each day is a new start to what lies ahead.
     Put your cares and your troubles behind.
Come join the parade and celebrate life.
     See what you can find.

Open your eyes, greet each day with a song.
     You've a whole new world to explore.
It's there for the taking, just hold on tight.
     It's right outside your door.

Today Only Once

Live for today; it only comes once,
    So enjoy it while you can.
Yesterday is gone and is history.
    Tomorrow we make a new plan.

Today is the first day of the rest of your life,
    A most important day.
A chance to correct mistakes you've made
    And find a better way.

Today's the tomorrow you dreamt of yesterday
    And thought might never come.
So live each moment to the fullest
    As you march to a different drum.

Be Yourself

Follow your dreams wherever they lead.
Watch your imagination soar.
Blaze a path that others may follow.
Be the leader that others look for.

Don't be content to follow the crowd.
Strike out on your own.
Learn to stand on your own two feet,
Then half the battle is won.

Be the person you were meant to be.
Leave the other you behind.
Search to find your inner strength.
Give yourself a chance to shine.

Obsessed

You may not know the man I've become,
    But I was the richest man alive.
Statues and buildings were named for me.
    Making money was my drive.

I had no time for others.
    Charity, I hadn't any.
Others have it; get it from them.
    I needed every penny.

My obsession became my downfall.
    Giving should have been my goal.
Now I'm on the bottom looking up,
    And I'm paying with my soul.

Seldom Noticed

I know it's not said often enough
  But thank you for all you do.
You do so much for others,
  Someone should recognize you.

No job is too small for you to do.
  You seem to be everywhere.
You do much more than nursing,
  But unless you're needed, who knows you're there?

There's only one you, so try to relax.
  Take a nice refreshing lunch.
Recharge your batteries and realize,
  You can only do so much.

Starting Point

Blaze a trail for others to follow.
    Set an example by what you do.
Show to the world the joy that it brings
    And that they can do it too.

Be a guiding light to someone in need,
    Or be someone's shining star.
Be someone's guardian angel
    No matter where you are.

You can be an example to family and friends
    When you open up your heart.
Giving a hand to any stranger you meet
    Is a perfect place to start.

Recharge

When your energy begins to fade
It's time you realize
You have to sit and rest a while
Or you're in for a big surprise.

Let your batteries charge and begin anew.
There's a whole new you within.
Relax your mind and just unwind.
That's when the healing begins.

After a while you'll feel refreshed;
Your life will start anew.
And the first thing you'll notice about this
Is you'll be a better you.

Why Change

Fingers do my talking; I lost my gift of speech.
    Wheels replaced my legs years ago.
Though some may think I'd carry a grudge,
    I'm the happiest person to know.

A heart still beats within my chest;
    My mind is active still.
I may be down, but I'm never out.
    And don't think I ever will.

I'm happy with the life I've had,
    And that's the way that it should be.
I have no reason to ever slow down.
    I'm too busy being me.

Admit, Open, Ask

Would you want to stop and rest awhile?
     I can see you're in distress.
We can talk if you like or just sit still
     But it will give you a chance to rest.

Neither spoke for a while, then he started to cry.
     He said, "I'm ashamed of things I've done.
I've lied and cheated, and look at me now.
     My life's starting to come undone."

I told him that it's never too late.
     You already admitted your sins.
Now all that's left is to open your heart
     And ask for Christ to come in.

Never Give Up

Although I face my struggles alone,
     I have the courage to see them through.
I know I have an inner strength
     To help me in anything I do.

I'll keep on trying when others have quit.
     My knees may buckle but they'll never bend.
If I need to, I'll call on my inner strength
     And keep moving to the end.

I won my fight; I didn't give up
     When my critics wanted me to.
I felt I could win and come out on top
     And you can do it too.

Within You

When one door closes, you just turn around
　　And find another way.
Just seek a new direction in life
　　To make it through the day.

When the going gets tough, you don't give up;
　　You hold your head up high.
Meet your troubles face to face
　　And give it another try.

You have it deep within you
　　To be all you wanted to be.
All you need is determination
　　And the courage to set it free.

Completed

It took some time, but you hit your mark.
　　You always knew you would.
When others considered you all washed up
　　You proved to them you could.

Though the struggle was hard, you never gave up.
　　You listened to within.
The voice of reason kept pushing you on
　　And told you you're going to win.

You're standing now at the finish line;
　　You ran your race, and won.
It's time to relax; your journey is over.
　　There's another race just begun.

A Blessing

Blessings

May you greet everyone as a neighbor
    With happiness and good cheer.
Invite them to sit by the fire
    For there are no strangers here.

May your life be full of laughter,
    Your heart be full of love.
May you find true peace and contentment,
    With blessings from above.

May you find your true calling in giving;
    Give freely to those that lack.
Give to those that are needy
    And may you never look back.

Stop and Refresh

When was the last time you rested awhile,
    Sat back and just reclined,
Listened to music or read a book,
    And took a trip inside your mind?

You'll find yourself enjoying this leisure time
    That rekindles memories of the past,
Wanting to return again and again,
    Hoping the time will last.

After a while you'll feel refreshed
    And ready to start anew.
Or you could keep going and run out of steam.
    The choice is up to you.

Never Let Go

Hold on tightly to those you love;
    Someday they won't be there.
You'll no longer have their company,
    No one with which to share.

Never take for granted the friends you have.
    You're liable to blink and they're gone.
Never miss a chance to offer thanks
    For everything they've done.

Someday you may find you're by yourself
    Wishing to see again
People you remembered from long ago
    Or the smiling face of a friend.

If Someone Needs You

Be to someone a guiding light;
    Help them find their way.
When someone's down, help build them up.
    Help them make it through the day.

When someone is hurting, be a comfort and joy;
    Be there if they need an ear.
Give them a shoulder if they need to cry;
    Tell them you'll try to be near.

It may not be easy helping others in need
    But you'll feel better inside
Knowing you helped your fellow man
    Or knowing at least you tried.

Responsibility Is Yours

Build your life how you want it to be;
    Make it yours and yours alone.
Don't pattern it after somebody else;
    Be ready to step out on your own.

Don't be molded by someone else;
    You have to make your own way.
You're responsible for what you chose
    And will answer for it one day.

You're one of a kind; choose your own style,
    Different than anyone else.
Choose one that tells people who you are.
    Don't be like others; be yourself.

My Wish for You

If there's one wish that I could make
    To protect you from all strife,
I wish you find your inner strength
    To last throughout your life.

I wish that you should find in you
    The will to carry on,
The courage to build a better life
    When you face the world alone.

But most of all I'd wish for you
    A happy, open heart,
A world where all can live as one
    And each can play a part.

Make a Chain

Instead of a circle, forge a chain.
    Don't just return a favor pass it on.
In time the chain will continue to grow,
    Hopefully from what you've begun.

The minute you give without wanting back
    The chain begins to grow.
The next person in line does the same
    And from there nobody knows.

Some find it hard to form a chain;
    They'd rather take than give.
They never did favors for anyone;
    They've forgotten how to live.

Ease Your Mind

When you find yourself in the pit of despair
And you're not sure what to do,
Don't listen to others who think they know;
Just do what's best for you.

There are self-help books by the dozens,
All guaranteeing a cure.
You try them out but soon realize
You're no better off than before.

The only way to ease your mind
And to find a little peace
Is to simply keep busy, help when you can,
And soon your worrying will cease.

Keep Moving Forward

I can't go back and change the past,
       But I can change what is to be.
The only way to make this happen
       Is by simply changing me.

I can choose to be a more confident self,
       Unafraid to stand on my own,
Be more positive in my outlook on life
       As I face the world alone.

Helping others should be my goal in life,
       Giving should be my aim.
'Til I get my life where I think it should be
       I'll never be the same.

Choose Kindness

Though fully grown, I'm a child at heart
So yes, I tend to believe
That people at heart are truly kind
As long as they choose to be.

Most have forgotten how to wear a smile
Or lend a helping hand.
Some refuse to help if asked
So they'll never understand.

Come show how kind you can truly be
By extending a hand to a friend.
Or make a friend of someone unknown
And bring their troubles to an end.

Satisfied with Yourself

If you look in the mirror each morning
     Are you satisfied with the view?
It matters not what others think
     As long as you're satisfied with you.

Look longer at the face you see
     To the person who is inside.
See if there are imperfections
     That you've been trying to hide.

The person you see each morning
     Is the same as others see.
Be happy with the person you are;
     You're the best you're going to be.

No Small Favors

Don't minimize your effort
     Or make the effect seem small.
It's the fact that you are even trying
     That will be remembered most of all.

If you think what you've been doing
     Means nothing to those you help out,
Think what they were like before you came.
     You'll see there isn't a doubt.

Always be happy with what you do;
     It's the effort that shows in the end
No matter how small the favor is,
     You're always a winner, my friend.

Really Not Bad

Every day I see people in pain
      And yet they continue to smile.
Each step they take seems like agony
      So I asked to talk a while.

I asked them why so happy
      When with each step you'd want to cry.
"It's not that bad" they tell themselves.
      "There are those worse off than I."

So next time you feel you want to complain
      Remember those worse off than you.
You'll realize your life is not that bad
      And you'll think before you do.

Helping Out

To those you help you're an answered prayer
Sent to ease their pain.
Even if it's only once in a while
They hope you'll come again.

It matters not how much you do
Or how much you're able to give,
They feel the effects and are grateful
That you're helping them try to live.

You'll feel better in the long run
Every time you open your heart.
Never miss a chance to make a smile
And help someone get a new start.

Special Feeling

Never miss a chance to share a smile,
    Help someone out, or make a friend.
Be willing to go that extra mile
    To bring their troubles to an end.

It doesn't take much to be a friend,
    All it takes is a little time.
If you lend an ear to those alone
    Everything will be fine.

The happiness you'll feel inside
    Hasn't been realized yet.
Your reward for helping others
    Is the feeling that you get.

Thankful for All

Always be thankful for what you have.
　　　There are those who wish they had
The little bit that you have got,
　　　So things really aren't that bad.

Be always thankful for the rain
　　　That falls upon the fields.
Be thankful when you sit to taste
　　　The harvest that it yields.

Be most thankful that you have life
　　　And friends with which to share.
Be thankful God watches over us
　　　And that he'll always care.

Down to Size

If the mountain seems too high to climb
    Just take it down a bit.
Rest for a while if the going gets tough;
    What you mustn't do is quit.

You'll never get anywhere by giving up
    And saying it can't be done.
Tell yourself you know you can
    And the battle is already won.

Look at all you've accomplished by trying
    And seeing things through to the end.
By not saying no and giving up
    You're a better person, my friend.

Follow Their Example

Just like us they had a dream
    And had a goal in sight.
They headed off to an unseen land
    To do what they felt was right.

They had no idea what they would find,
    But they knew what they were leaving.
To fulfill that dream they followed their heart
    To a freedom they were given.

Like our ancestors of long ago
    You too must follow your dream.
You'll find like them that it can be done;
    It isn't as crazy as it seems.

Believe It's True

Keep telling yourself you're a failure
      And you'll convince yourself that you are.
Keep looking at things in a negative way
      And you'll never get very far.

It depends on how you see yourself
      That determines what you do.
You could be a winner or a failure;
      The choice is up to you.

So, though you may be down for now
      You're stronger than you know.
You're never a failure if you never give up
      But you have to believe it's so.

Each Day

Greet each day with a song in your heart
    Despite what the weather might bring.
Forget what happened yesterday;
    That's the most important thing.

Say hello to the people you meet,
    Greet everyone by name,
Be they rich or poor, it matters not.
    Treat everyone the same.

Find more pleasure in the beauties of life;
    Relax whenever you can.
Stop for a while amongst the trees;
    Be a friend to man.

Be Ready

You have it within you to do many things
    If only you feel you can,
But no matter how good your intentions
    You must start out with a plan.

Make a plan to follow your heart
    No matter where it may lead,
Always putting others first,
    Helping those in need.

It's always good to plan for the future,
    Though keep open for what may hide.
Dreams may come and dreams may go;
    They're as changing as the tide.

Be Someone's Something

Though you have your problems you're always there
Every time someone needs a friend.
Maybe they'll need a shoulder to cry on
Or just someone to understand.

Maybe you'll be their guiding light
And help to light the way.
You may prove to be the ray of hope
That will help them through the day.

Whatever may be your lot in life,
To help your fellow man,
Have no regrets with what you do;
Just be the best you can.

Make It Real

You set a goal now make a plan
    To make that dream come true.
Never lose sight of the finish line
    Whatever you have to do.

You may have trials along the line
    But don't let them get in the way.
Set your eyes upon the prize
    And know you'll get there someday.

The goal may be only just a dream,
    One you may never know.
Unless you possess the courage to try
    And the will to make it so.

May It Be?

May the New Year bring you happiness
    And the start of something good.
May it be the start of a whole new life?
    Living as you should.

May it be a year to forget your past?
    And all the troubles it brought.
But never forget the things you've learned
    Through the lessons that it taught.

May it prove to be a happier year
    That finds you better at the end.
And may next year be even better yet
    Because you deserve it, my friend.

Happier Days

Close your eyes and try to relax;
　　　　Let your cares go drifting away.
Feel yourself floating on billowing clouds
　　　　As you return to yesterday.

Return to the days when you were a child;
　　　　You were always happier then.
Mom and Dad were the center of your world;
　　　　Brothers and sisters your closest friends.

I open my eyes; those days are gone
　　　　But the memories remain
To visit me from time to time
　　　　And be relived again and again.

Well Lived

May your life be a beacon for others
    That they may see the light.
Always set an example for others to follow
    To know what's wrong from right.

Always pass your wisdom to others
    So they too may know what you know.
Always be ready to share a smile
    To light a spark wherever you go.

Be glad if your life was not in vain;
    That you did all that you could;
That you helped someone else to see the light
    And that's more than others would.

Hang On and Believe

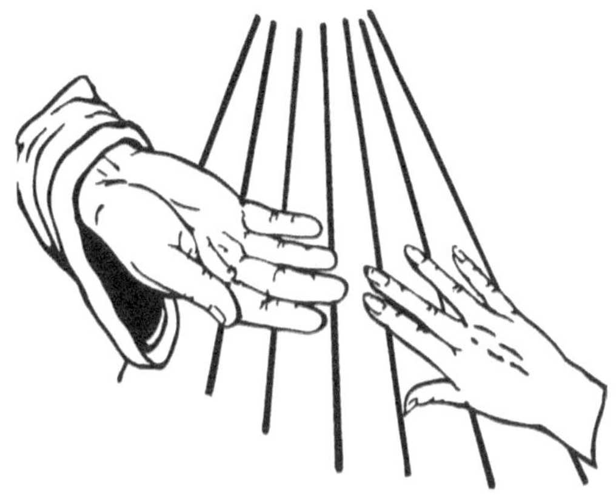

Don't give up; you're an integral part
    Of what God has in store.
You've so much to pass to those next in line
    With all you've learned so far.

You were never promised an easy life
    But you are promised that He'd care.
Don't be afraid to call His name,
    He promised He'd always be there.

You may not believe in who He is,
    Or even what He can do.
But rest assured no matter what,
    He believes in you.

Forget Them for Now

If you want to feel like you're helping,
      You have to forget about self.
Take all the time you spend on you
      And spend it on somebody else.

Lend a hand to a friend unexpectedly
      Or help a child with a task.
The elderly always need a listening ear
      Without having to be asked.

When you open your heart to others,
      Your troubles will all fade away.
I'm not saying you don't still have them,
      But you'll face them another day.

All That Is Needed

You may never be as strong as some,
        Ready to lead men.
That doesn't mean you're not at the front
        Doing the best you can.

You have inside you the courage
        And the willingness to defend
When it comes to the aid of your country
        Or helping to protect a friend.

You may never be a leader of men,
        Or one to make history.
To those who matter, a trusting friend
        Might be all you'll ever be.

About the Author

Charles was born in 1953, the third of seven sons. He was born with cerebral palsy and seizures. He started writing when he was in high school, but he started writing seriously after graduating in 1971. That's when he started volunteering with an organization to help handicapped individuals. He started writing about their trials and how they overcame them. In 1987 he became a Special Olympics bowling coach.

He lives in Lansdale, Pennsylvania.